Donal Neary SJ

COMMUNION
FOR
SUNDAYS AND HOLY DAYS

YEAR A

VERITAS

First published by
Veritas Publications
7-8 Lower Abbey Street
Dublin 1

ISBN 1 85390 233 0

Cover design by Banahan McManus
Printed in the Republic of Ireland by Criterion Press Ltd, Dublin

CONTENTS

Introduction 5

Season of Advent 7

Season of Christmas 14

Season of Lent 19

Season of Easter 25

Ordinary Time 39

Holy Days 82
   The Immaculate Conception 82
   The Epiphany of the Lord 83
   St Patrick 85
   The Ascension of the Lord 86
   The Body and Blood of Christ 87
   The Assumption of Mary 89
   All Saints 91

INTRODUCTION

Communion Reflections for Sundays and Holy Days of Year A presents short reflections, mostly based on the scripture of the day, which are suitable for reading after communion. Sometimes the reflection is centred on the feast of the day or a general aspect of the Christian life, for example, the reflection for the Feast of the Immaculate Conception is a prayerful meditation on Mary. Now and then a general reflection has been used, as in a 'Prayer for Every Day' for the Twenty-second Sunday in Ordinary Time.

Many people have noted that the Mass can 'end very suddenly', and there is need for a wide variety of reflections which may sum up and link in the readings, theme of the feast and the Mass. They value highly the inclusion of a Communion reflection, read in the quiet time and space of the Mass after Communion has finished, not while people are on the way to Communion.

On reading the Communion reflection

In introducing people to reading the Communion reflection, some attention might be paid to the differences between reading meditations, praying a prayer, preaching a homily, proclaiming the Scripture.

A Communion reflection is to be shared, rather than proclaimed or preached. This affects the tone of voice, the mood communicated through reading, the speed of reading and the way of preparation. It will be read slowly. In cases where some line of the Scripture is repeated, two voices might be used. Repetitions of words will be noted, as they then sink into the heart. 'Gently', 'softly', 'prayerfully' and 'slowly' are words the reader of the Communion reflection might recall when reading and preparing to read.

Careful preparation is more necessary for Communion reflections than for other liturgical readings, which may be more familiar. The Communion reflection is new both to reader and listener, and thus needs careful and prayerful preparation. The reader of a Communion reflection should have the text well in advance of a liturgy and have time to pray over it.

Many people find the use of music in the background to Communion reflections intrusive. Others find it creates a mood of reflection. If music is used in the background, it needs to be such that does not distract from the reflection. Thus, an instrumental played too loudly or the music of a well-known hymn can distract from the content of the Communion reflection.

Communion Reflections For Sundays and Holy Days of Year A may also be used for private prayer; many of the reflections might be used also on other liturgical occasions, fitting simlar themes or Scripture readings. May they enhance the liturgy with personal reflection on the great mysteries of our faith and thus bring the reader personally closer to the Lord Jesus, whose death and resurrection is the theme of every Christian liturgy.

Donal Neary SJ

FIRST SUNDAY OF ADVENT

Waiting

You are always there
In a quiet room
Waiting for me
To come to you.

This morning in
A hilly field,
Sitting on the corner
Of a stone cattle trough,
Listening to the water
Tumbling down the hill
Into the silent river,
Watching the crows
Fly to work
Across the sky,
Why was I surprised
To find you there?

Lord, teach me
To leave space
In my mind
So that you
Can always be there.

Alice Taylor, 'Praying Place'

SECOND SUNDAY OF ADVENT

He will make his home among us.

We need a place we call home;
where there is acceptance,
a place we can just be ourselves.
Home is the place of family, friendship and of faith.
In the love of family, we find we can be ourselves,
and relax into the mystery of being loved for who we are,
and that is what home is.
In the love of friendship we also find our home,
accepted and affirmed for who we are,
loved for what is strong and weak within us.
And in faith there is the love of God,
accepting, affirming, forgiving all we are and need.

He will make his home among us.

Home is more than bricks and mortar,
more than a garden and a house;
it is the place of warmth and acceptance.

And Jesus said to many he met
'Today I want to stay in your house'.
He makes his home within you,
in the warmth of your heart and
in the centre of your personality,
bringing with him
gifts of affirmation, affection,
acceptance and forgiveness.

He will make his home among us.

THIRD SUNDAY OF ADVENT

Building the Kingdom

Have you ever watched children building bricks?
as they sit there, they are at work and play.
Look at the wonder in their faces as they build.
They are building their dreams.

Their eyes are closed with determination.
'I'll do it this time,' they are thinking.
They smile as they place each brick,
and this is the joy of learning.

Look at their gentle hands,
they are the hands
of a carpenter,
of a healer,
of a peace-maker,
of a creator.
Each brick is precious,
it is handled with care.

Let's learn from these children,
as we work to build our lives
and the kingdom of God.
May we plan and design with hope and care,
may we always use our Christian materials,
the bricks of love,
the sands of tolerance,
the waters of faith.

John McHugh

FOURTH SUNDAY OF ADVENT

Joseph, do not be afraid to take Mary home as your wife.

Isn't it a story of faith?

Joseph, wondering and afraid of what was going on in
    Mary?
Mary, afraid of her call to be the mother of God?

Fear and faith go together.
You believe in a person and maybe you'll be let down.
You believe in God and you can't pin him down.
So much of life is lived in trust:
that love once promised will last,
that children will be safe and will do the right thing,
that health will last and old age will be safe;
we want our security.

And Mary and Joseph were the same;
wanting security in relationship and religion.
And their real safety was in God.

Do not be afraid, the Lord says;
I am your companion all your days.
And Jesus who became a man in Palestine,
is with us today in bread and wine.

**Joseph, do not be afraid to take Mary home as your
    wife.**

CHRISTMAS VIGIL

**Glory to God in the highest
and peace to his people on earth.**

> This is the night of reconciliation; let us be neither
> wrathful nor gloomy on it.
> On this all-peaceful night let us be neither menacing nor
> boisterous.
> This is the night of the Gentle One; let us be on it
> neither bitter nor harsh.
> On this night of the Humble One, let us be neither
> proud nor haughty.
> On this day of forgiveness let us not avenge offences.
> On this day of rejoicings let us not share sorrows.
> On this sweet day let us not be vehement.
> On this calm day let us not be quick-tempered.
> On this day the the Rich One was made poor for our sake,
> let the rich also make the poor sharers at their tables.
> On this day a gift came without our asking for it,
> let us then give alms to those who cry out and beg from us.
> This is the day when the high gate opened to us for our
> prayers...

**Glory to God in the highest
and peace to his people on earth.**

St Ephrem of Syria

CHRISTMAS DAY

The day of the Child

Our hearts go out to a child.
No matter what the circumstances of birth,
our heart is enlarged by a child.

There is no such thing as an unwanted child.
Every child – one-parent family, separated family,
unmarried or married parents –
is wanted and welcomed by God.

And Jesus in the crib represents all the children of the
    world.
Small and loved.
Then big in the love of God.
Everyone is important in the crib of Bethlehem –
not because of good looks, money, sport,
race or religion.

You are important because you are you.
All of us are important in the crib of Bethlehem.

Haven't we many ways of valuing each other?
Looking up to people for their jobs,
valuing them for their families or property,
or the influence they have in our locality?

Isn't that all so empty?

Loved for who you are.
The crib means God loves you.
Also that God saves you.

We need to hear this message; the real voice of Christmas.
To see the baby loved by God
in the love of Mary and Joseph,
and to hear from God the real Christmas message,
you're loved, you are forgiven.

He sees and loves in us
what he sees and loves in Jesus.

A CHRISTMAS MEDITATION AT THE CRIB

As we place Joseph in the crib, we place with him all men: we pray for the men we love and worry about; husbands, brothers, grandsons, sons, friends and others; and especially we place fathers in the crib, from whom we get life and identity. We remember men who are silently suffering hardships for their children and wives, for men who are emotionally starved and, especially, for those who are unemployed.

As we place Mary in the crib, we remember women: wives, sisters, daughters, granddaughters, friends; we remember mothers, giving life to their children as Mary gave life to Jesus. We remember women who are victims of violence in the home, exploitation in the workplace and sexual exploitation, and women who are in any way victimised because they are women.

As we place the shepherds in the crib, we remember people who are looked down on in society; may we show compassion and care for the poor of our parish and city; for prisoners and others looked down on in society; for all who have been victimised or abused in any way; we remember also all who suffer in the cause of justice and human rights throughout the world.

As we place Jesus in the crib, we remember children – our own children and young people whom we know and love. We remember children who, like Jesus, are born poor and homeless. We remember children who are victims of physical or sexual abuse, or who, through no fault of their own, do not have a good start in life.

As we place Jesus, Mary and Joseph in the crib, we place ourselves and know that we have our place there with them. May each person here have a happy Christmas. Comfort those who mourn, console those who are worried, give peace to our world.

FEAST OF THE HOLY FAMILY

An ordinary family

In some of the ordinary experiences of family life,
Jesus grew up from childhood.

In the love of Joseph and Mary
he learned to trust that they would care for him,
he learned to pray,
he learned of his people's faith.

He knew the joys of family life:
Mary and Joseph's wedding anniversary,
his own birthday and schooling,
and knew the joy of their pride in him.
They taught him how to grow up
through adolescence and early adult life,
growing as he did in wisdom.

And they wondered about him
as parents wonder about their children –
how he would turn out,
and all that was said about him.

He knew some of family life's sorrows;
the death of grandparents,
the death of Joseph,
the struggle to make ends meet,
and leaving home to find his own path in life.

This son of Mary and Joseph was God;
but that was hidden from them;
their family life was a hidden life,
and in that hidden life,
the mission of Jesus became visible.

May the ordinary life of the family
of Mary, Joseph and Jesus,
give us hope and courage,
in times when family life is really tough
and we know we must entrust others to life and to God;
may it give us hope and courage too
in the ordinary ups and downs
of our own family life.

SUNDAY AFTER CHRISTMAS

Come and see

The searcher in us wants to see what the Lord has to offer: **come and see.**

We want peace in our hearts, freedom from fears and anxieties: **come and see.**

We want to know that life is forever, and that love is worthwhile, even when we feel our life and love are wasted: **come and see.**

We want to know that someone cares all the time for the poor and the needy: **come and see.**

We want to be sure that God is kind and loving and is as close to us as he says he is: **come and see.**

We want to know that the mystery we call God is in the middle of all the mysteries of human life: **come and see.**

We want to know that one day there will be life and joy forever and we will hear from Jesus: **come and see.**

BAPTISM OF THE LORD

You are my son, my daughter, the beloved

You are amazed that God could say to you,
You are my son, my daughter, the beloved.

You feel ashamed of your past,
You are my son, my daughter, the beloved.

You are afraid of the future, of illness, of uselessness and
   of death,
You are my son, my daughter, the beloved.

You are guilty for what you've said about another,
You are my son, my daughter, the beloved.

You criticise others in word and thought and judgement,
   and know that God says of each person,
You are my son, my daughter, the beloved.

You feel bad about yourself, how you look, how you feel,
You are my son, my daughter, the beloved.

You rejoice in your talents, your gifts, and the love of
   your life,
You are my son, my daughter, the beloved.

You are grateful for the friendship of others and you
   know that God says of each of them,
You are my son, my daughter, the beloved.

You wonder about God and search for him in the
   questions of your life,
You are my son, my daughter, the beloved.

FIRST SUNDAY OF LENT

The Spirit of God

The Spirit of God tells us that we should fast,
because it will awaken us to our own poverty
and to the many millions of people
who do not have enough to eat.

The Spirit of God calls us in the season of Lent
to renew our baptismal promise
to live a Christian life of faith, hope and love.

The Spirit of God reminds us
that we are responsible for everyone, everywhere,
until the end of time.

The Spirit of God challenges us
to live a life of forgiveness,
for this is the only way to be set free
from the overwhelming power of sin.

The Spirit of God whispers in our hearts
that wealth and appearance,
background and prestige are not important –
everyone is worthwhile, lovable
and to be cherished simply because they are alive.

The Spirit of God embraces the sick and the handicapped,
for people who are deeply aware of their limitations
are often the people who are most alive.

The Spirit of God believes that the great spirit of life
is not quenched in death,
but is transformed into a new and deeper life.

SECOND SUNDAY OF LENT

And they saw his glory

> They saw his glory and were surprised.
> We see his glory all around us
> and often do not notice it,
> and when we do notice it,
> we are surprised.
>
> Christ in the surprise of a January flower,
> Christ in the discovery of new love,
> Christ in the offering and welcoming of reconciliation,
> Christ in the tireless efforts of men and women of peace,
>
> In the schoolroom in a city slum
> where a teacher for a low salary
> transforms the lives of the poor
> who are God's favourites,
>
> **And they saw his glory**
> in the efforts to free those imprisoned unjustly
> by regimes which feed their own greed,
>
> in the hours of listening in a marriage,
> in the time spent watching in love over a sick child,
> in caring for the sick, the lonely, the old,
> in all those times
> we go out of our own cares, big or small,
> to enter the cares of others.
>
> **And they saw his glory:**
> and in such moments
> we too see his glory.

THIRD SUNDAY OF LENT

**Anyone who drinks the water that I will give
will never be thirsty again.**

> So much in life we want, desire, need:
> food and drink,
> friendship and love,
> sex and acceptance;
> Jesus, what have you to offer?
> What does it mean that
> **Anyone who drinks the water that I will give
> will never be thirsty again?**
>
> Human wants and desires are confused;
> we want happiness and look in the wrong places;
> we're like the woman at the well,
> looking for happiness in a place we can't find it,
> and open to the love Jesus offers:
> **Anyone who drinks the water that I will give
> will never be thirsty again.**
>
> I thank you Lord, for faith,
> for the roots of my life which nobody else can give;
> I thank you for a meaning in life
> which makes me strong from birth to death;
> I thank you for the Eucharist
> which nourishes all life's moments;
> I thank you for forgiveness,
> which means I need never stay stuck in faults.
>
> Thank you for this living water:
> **Anyone who drinks the water that I will give
> will never be thirsty again.**

FOURTH SUNDAY OF LENT

I am the light of the world, says the Lord.
Anyone who follows me will have the light of life.

> Our life with God
> is a journey,
> sometimes uphill, other times level,
> through light and shadow,
> to the fullness of God's eternal joy.

> It is a journey,
> sometimes gentle, sometimes strenuous,
> through doubt and faith,
> to the fullness of God's eternal life.

> It is a journey,
> sometimes solitary, other times accompanied,
> through isolation and love,
> to the fullness of God's eternal friendship.

> It is a journey,
> sometimes sad, sometimes joyful,
> through sorrows and happiness,
> to the fullness of God's eternal joy.

I am the light of the world, says the Lord.
Anyone who follows me will have the light of life.

FIFTH SUNDAY OF LENT

From death to life

What a way to receive great glory:
to die!

Jesus paints a picture of death and life –
the ears of corn ripening colourfully in the air of God,
these will be life-giving food – a miracle of God.
And when the grain dies and falls into the earth,
it multiplies, nourishes even more than before.

The glory of the grain of wheat begins when it's buried in clay,
the glory of Jesus begins on the cross.

The glory of a person is in dying to
the false self,
the arrogant self,
the grasping self,
and rising in the love of God
in truth, humility, sharing.

We rise and die each day
as we are called forth in the resurrection of Jesus
to show to people
the victory of Jesus in love over hate,
in reconciliation over bitterness,
in faith over despair.

Lord Jesus,
die in us,
rise in us,
that we in you may serve our Father.

PASSION SUNDAY

He was not crucified alone,
and he is not crucified alone today.

> We're all part of Jesus,
> he has no body now but ours.
> he suffers today in his people,
> and he suffers in you.

He was not crucified alone,
and he is not crucified alone today.

> Are you ill? He suffers in your illness.
> Are you lonely? He suffers in your loneliness.
> Are you homeless? He suffers in your homelessness.
> Have you been neglected? He suffers in your neglect.
> Have you been abused? He suffers in your abuse.
> Have you been despairing? He suffers in your despair.
> Are you victimised by greed? He suffers with you.

> He has no body now on earth but yours.

> He was consoled by the look of Mary – his mother,
> by the touch of Veronica – his consoler,
> by the helping hand of Simon – his cross-carrier,
> by the quiet presence of John – his friend.

> You are Jesus.

> And you are Mary, Veronica, Simon, John,
> his helpers on the way of the Cross.

> You are the body of Christ.

He was not crucified alone,
and he is not crucified alone today.

EASTER SUNDAY

They have taken the Lord out of the tomb.

She had come back to the tomb,
a woman who missed Jesus,
as we visit the graves of our loved ones.

She couldn't wait and arrived in the darkness.
And don't we often go to God in our darkness?

Our darkness of grief, doubt, sadness;
the days we feel downcast, let-down,
hopeless about a job,
anxious about a child,
worried over an exam;
we go to God in our deadness and darkness.

Like Mary going to the tomb;
something had died in her
when Jesus died.

In her darkness she went
where she would find some hope:
to the tomb of the One who gave her life.

And she found life again; but not immediately.
Maybe then there were glimmers of hope,
like joy returning slowly at times in life.
With the disciples who gradually recognised
that his promise of rising again was true,
she knew again the light and the joy she once had.

We go to the tomb of Jesus in our own darkness,
in our hope that peace, courage and good times will
     follow.
Let Easter nourish our faith,
increase our hope,

and keep alive our love
that the Lord is risen.

Nobody took the Lord out of the tomb!
He was raised from death by God his Father.
He is risen indeed.
Like the apostles may we believe this truly;
He is risen indeed,
Alleluia.

SECOND SUNDAY OF EASTER

Blessed are they who have not seen and yet believe.

> That's you and me,
> and the millions who have believed in Jesus
> on the strength of the gospel and his life.

> Blessed are they
> who have seen the consistent love of parents
> and know that Jesus is alive;
> who have known the care for years of a spouse
> and know that Jesus is alive;
> who have spent generous hours with the poor,
> and know that Jesus is alive.

Blessed are they who have not seen and yet believe.

> And who can look at a flower and be reminded of Jesus'
>   risen life,
> 'who see his blood upon the rose,
> and in the stars the glory of his eyes'.

Blessed are they who have not seen and yet believe.

> And who see in the lined faces of the hungry, the face of
>   Christ;
> who hear in the cry of the homeless for shelter, the cry of
>   Christ;
> who feel for the loneliness of those who feel lost, the
>   abandonment of Christ;

Blessed are they who have not seen and yet believe.

> In our Eucharist, Lord Jesus,
> let us recognise our need for you,
> let us wince at the needs of the poor,
> let us glimpse the joy of eternity.

Blessed are they who have not seen and yet believe.

THIRD SUNDAY OF EASTER

We had been hoping.

How often we've said or thought that:
We had been hoping.

That love would last or a relationship would get deeper,
that illness would ease or death would be delayed,
that employment would come or a raise would be
    offered,
that life would be enjoyable, comfortable:
We had been hoping.

And there have been disappointments:
let-downs by friends, by family,
promotions not found in a job,
success in exams lost,
prayers not answered,
love lost or not found.

How to get through this?
The apostles had put faith in Jesus,
had invested much of their lives in him.
Their disappointment blocked their faith in his
    resurrection.

We had been hoping.

Yes, it was ordained that glory comes through suffering;
there's the love and growth and fullness
discovered even in disappointment.
Even in the darkness of disappointment,
do we not find glimpses of light?
And we know in the heart
that nothing except love is lasting.

He vanished from their sight,
but left the Eucharist;
a sure sign
that no disappointment is final.
that there is always hope,
and the possibility of new life.

Was it not ordained that
I should suffer
and so enter into glory?

FOURTH SUNDAY OF EASTER

I have come that you may have life to the full.

One of the titles of God
is 'Lover of Life'.

God is the lover of
real life among us;
yet we often make him into a killjoy God.

Jesus brought the life of
forgiveness to people crippled with guilt,
peace to those driven by anxiety,
hope to people darkened by despair,
friendship to people isolated in loneliness:

Jesus' gift of life
is the gift of love.
His companionship offers
peace, forgiveness, hope,
in all the experiences of life.

I have come that you may have life to the full.

Lord, lover of life,
make us truly grateful
for gifts of laughter and humour,
of endurance and courage,
of care and reconciliation,
and for all which makes us truly alive.

I have come that you may have life to the full.

FIFTH SUNDAY OF EASTER

I am the Way, the Truth and the Life.

The Way that guides our steps, another name for the
    Lord Jesus.
Like a path guides us through a forest in the mist,
the Lord guides our way in life.
He has walked our ways before:
knowing bereavement and failure,
knowing rejection and poverty,
knowing loneliness and loss of faith.

He is the Truth that enlightens our mind;
like a glimpse of light in the fog;
he gives meaning in times of emptiness,
some experiences of peace in confusion,
and certainty that we can find the Truth of Life
in the gospel of his Father.

And he is the Life.
He gives hope and comfort in our yearnings for fullness,
he gives a confidence that the biggest gift of all is life,
and that in emptiness and in pain,
in doubt and confusion,
he offers a new surge of life,
the life that comes from knowing
that we are loved intensely
and called to love as best we can in life.

Thus we live in
the way, the truth, and the life of God,
in Jesus Christ,
for he says,
I am the Way, the Truth and the Life.

SIXTH SUNDAY OF EASTER

To be a people of hope

From the very beginning of our existence,
from our first whispering cries,
we struggle to make sense
of who we are and what we are
and of the strange, new furniture of our lives,
of sounds and smells, of warmth and cold,
of light and shadow, of hands and faces;
to put together
the bits and pieces of our experience
into some kind of order,
so that we may live without fear
in the midst of powers and forces
which overwhelm us.
We cry to one another,
'What have you discovered?
Do you know the way?'
and to those who have gone before,
'Let your light go on burning,
tell us your secrets.
Set out your experiences
in ways we can make our own',
lest we live like foreigners in the land,
alien to one another's ways,
strangers to the spoken word,
for to be human
is to live in a world of meaning;
but to live without meaning
is to be a stranger
to the human condition.

Anon

SEVENTH SUNDAY OF EASTER

**I pray for those you have given me,
because they belong to you.**

In the hour of Jesus' death,
you might wonder what was on his mind.
Did he wonder about the success of his mission,
or how his message would be spread?

Maybe, or maybe not.

But we do know that he prayed for his friends.
**I pray for those you have given me,
because they belong to you.**

From the supper room
where he looked at his friends,
with love and sadness in his heart,
he prayed for them, and assured them
that he would always be with them
in bread and wine.

And from the cross he looked
on all his friends,
who stood at a distance.
And he looked beyond his friends
to all who would believe in him.

**I pray for those you have given me,
because they belong to you.**

He prays for you now,
as he prayed for you then.
Praying like a father for a daughter,
a mother for a son,
a friend for a friend,
a grandparent for a grandchild.

Allow him to pray for you;
allow him to reach out to you in love,
for real prayer is to teach us
to love one another.
And join with his prayer
for those you wish to pray for.

**I pray for those you have given me,
because they belong to you.**

PENTECOST SUNDAY

As the Father sent me, so am I sending you.

Today we remember the birth of the Church,
the day we give thanks to God
for being part of the work of Jesus,
sent among us from the love of God,
sent within us to share the love of God.

The bravest of all life's calls is to love,
to say Yes to the call to love
husband or wife, children;
to say Yes to the call to love
the large family of God's people.

A call to all,
married, single,
priest, religious.

The birth of the Church
is like celebrating the birth of someone we love:
we celebrate who the person is,
not the ideal of what the person might be;
we give thanks for the person's past,
rejoice in another's present life,
and hope for the future.

We do that this day as Christians:
celebrate our Church as it is,
with its sinful members and its saints,
with its weak and its strong,
with its young and its old.

We celebrate the good done for many centuries
by people who took joyfully the words to their hearts,
As the Father sent me, so am I sending you.

And we want the Spirit of God
to refresh and renew within us
the desire we have
to receive and spread the love of God
wherever we can.

As the Father sent me, so am I sending you.

TRINITY SUNDAY

God so loved the world that he gave his only Son.

From their eternal home the Trinity look on our world.
Father, Son and Spirit,
they see that we need them.
We need to know more of the love of God,
and what is the true meaning of our lives.

They look on our world
and see our hungers and thirsts,
our homelessness and exile,
our unemployment and conflicts.
They see homes at peace and unhappy,
marriages needing help.
They see the confusion of the young,
the loneliness of the old.

Today's feast means they care.
That's what it means –
God so loved the world that he gave his only Son.

They sent the best help they knew to the people
they loved and who needed their help.
They sent not just a word of comfort,
or vague promises of help.
They sent one of themselves.
They sent Jesus;
God so loved the world that he gave his only Son.

And through Mary,
a young woman about to marry,
the word was made flesh.
Through millions since then
the love of the Trinity is alive in the world –
through you, through me,
in the love and the care we show,

in the faith we live by and the hope we share,
God so loved the world that he gave his only Son.

Let's give thanks for that great mystery:
Glory be…

SECOND SUNDAY IN ORDINARY TIME

Yes, I have seen that He is the Chosen One of God.

Did he look like that?
the man who queued up
to be baptised by John the Baptist?

Jesus of Nazareth,
a young man not unlike many others,
taking his place with sinners.

Like joining the line in a Penance Service,
or the crowd climbing a holy mountain for sins,
becoming one of the people
saying 'I am a sinner'.

Jesus saying, 'I am one of you'.

And John sees more:
the man of bright vision in front of him
his cousin he knew from their holidays together,
is the Son of God,
the One who should be baptising.

Yes, I have seen that He is the Chosen One of God.

Can you see, in the faces of the people around you,
the chosen ones of God?
Because of Jesus
we are all chosen ones of God.

In Jesus we see, not just the young man of Nazareth,
but every man and woman of every place,
and see in each of them, the chosen one of God.

THIRD SUNDAY IN ORDINARY TIME

Follow me.

> Lord, thanks for these words,
> I need to hear them.

Follow me.

> Words which echo in my heart.

> When I was younger
> and wondered about the consistent direction of my life,
> the words were there,
> gentle, persuasive, liberating –
> **Follow me.**

> When I wonder what I'll do with my life.
> In the doubts of how to give my time and love
> when the options were many,
> and some seemed more appealing than others –
> **Follow me.**

> When I wonder about the challenges of life,
> the needs of the poor in this unequal world,
> the abuse of the child and the vulnerable,
> the Church with its sinfulness and failings,
> the words still echo –
> **Follow me and I will make you fishers of people.**

> In the small ways that love challenges –
> the times for listening, for caring,
> for giving time, for a helping hand,
> with the people I'm with all the time,
> the words echo
> with their challenge and their comfort–
> **Come, follow me.**

Thanks, Lord for these words.
And I ask you that I will be open
always to hear them.

FOURTH SUNDAY IN ORDINARY TIME

You are blessed.

Strange that Jesus says that we are blessed
if we are poor, gentle, mourning, merciful, peacemakers.
Others might say we are blessed
if we are rich, tough and comfortable,
and looking for our own rights and desserts.

There is a blessing in all that he says:
not an immediate happiness nor prosperity,
but a blessing comes from God
in the times when we are weak, vulnerable, broken.

The bread of the Eucharist is bread broken and shared,
the blessing of God is mourning accepted and shared;
the blessing of God is mercy asked and given
so that the bread of the Eucharist is the bread of
       forgiveness,
and the blessing of God fills the places of the soul
where I am poor, lost, gentle,
and willing to let go of the grudges of life
for the life and resurrection of Jesus.

The closed fist cannot receive the gifts of life;
help us Lord, to be open
in our weakness and our need,
in our mourning and our bitterness
to the blessings you give
when we are disheartened.

Like in the Eucharist,
may we know your power and presence
in our broken dreams,
our broken relationships,
and rise to new strength within ourselves,
blessed as we are in the bread of life.

FIFTH SUNDAY IN ORDINARY TIME

You are the light of the world.

When you share your bread with the hungry,
You are the light of the world.

When you do your best to find shelter and homes for the
    poor,
You are the light of the world.

When you clothe those who are cold and educate those
    in ignorance,
or support those who help others,
You are the light of the world.

In the darkness of loneliness and of isolation,
the light of God will shine
only because you have chosen
to be a helper,
to be a carer,
to be a friend.

In the darkness and gloom of confusion and dread
the light of God will shine
only because you have chosen
to be a helper,
a listener,
a friend.

Let our words, Lord,
be words which bring light;
let our touch
bring consolation and light,
and let us believe,
strongly and in the heart,
that each of us is the light of God.

You are the light of the world.

SIXTH SUNDAY IN ORDINARY TIME

If your virtue goes no deeper than that of the scribes and Pharisees, you will never get into the kingdom of heaven.

You can do the right things for the wrong reason,
like going to Mass to be seen there, or to avoid God's
    displeasure,
like helping someone in school to look well for a teacher –
and then our virtue is no deeper than a hypocrite's.
We are people of mixed motivations,
and God wants our goodness to be sincere.
In the intention of the heart, God is pleased,
wanting our lives to be lived in love.
The smallest help to another done from love
is worth more than the biggest done to get approval;
that's what Jesus meant when he praised the poor woman
who gave away a small amount – all she had;
and what it means is that God never asks more than we
    can give.
And we can give everything away, even our bodies in
    death,
but if we have no love, it means nothing at all.
And what could look less than the piece of bread at Mass?
But this is God giving all of himself to us.
We ask for the gift of sincerity.

SEVENTH SUNDAY IN ORDINARY TIME

You must therefore be perfect just as your Heavenly Father is perfect.

To be perfect as God is perfect:
really, can we be like that?
The really perfect quality of God
is the love he has for each.

A love which
affirms, forgives, accepts,
enjoys, calls us,
day by day.

A love which strives for justice,
which wants to include everyone.
It's to be part of the circle of the love of God:
that's what being perfect seems to mean.

That you would have no faults,
nor think no evil,
nor fail in friendship;
Is that sometimes how we feel
God expects us to be,
a type of harsh, remote God,
'perfect in every way'?

'As the Father loves me,
so I love you...
love one another.'
This is the type of love which is God's perfect love.

Into that circle of love, the Lord invites you;
the love that you become part of,
a love that
affirms, forgives, accepts,
makes allowances,

strives for justice,
and that love is made perfect
because you and I want to be part of it.

**You must therefore be perfect just as your Heavenly
Father is perfect.**

EIGHTH SUNDAY IN ORDINARY TIME

I will never forget you.

To be remembered –
something we all like.
A letter, a Christmas card,
a photo in the kitchen,
a gift we gave to someone,
are ways of remembering
friends and family
and people dear to us.

And that's the way God thinks about each of us:
I will never forget you.

We wonder has love been forgotten,
has friendship been ignored,
and if we feel like that,
we feel diminished, lonely, unvalued.

It's good to know that God remembers us,
he compares his memory to a parent's,
a mother always remembering birth,
a father always remembering childhood,
the first smiles and the first words,
the first steps and the first falls;
remembering with love:
I will never forget you.

And if there are faults,
they are remembered only
with forgiveness and with love.

And isn't that what the daily bread and wine say:
each Eucharist is God's big statement
in the love of Jesus Christ:
I will never forget you.

NINTH SUNDAY IN ORDINARY TIME

Built on rock

No matter what our age,
we look for security;
we look for firm ground to stand on,
and that's what Jesus offers
when he says that his word is a rock
to live our lives by.

We live on firm ground
when we find love in our lives,
when we find meaning and direction,
when we find something
big enough to believe in
through all our experiences.

If we live by the word of Jesus,
we have firm ground,
our home is **built on rock**.

Be grateful for the rocks of your life:
for the people who have always been there for you,
for the love of God which never fails,
for the faith that can give direction to all of life.

Be grateful for fun and humour,
for laughter and for tears,
be grateful for the sun that sets daily,
for all this is beauty.
And when we notice beauty our home is **built on rock**.

Be grateful for the child that smiles or wakens you,
for the embrace that consoles or strengthens you,
for the joy that comes from saying sorry or making up.

Beauty, love, reconciliation –
all bits of firm ground for life,
and on this firm ground,
our home is **built on rock.**

TENTH SUNDAY IN ORDINARY TIME

God loves you at your weakest.

A saint once said,
looking back over his life,
'God loves you most when you love yourself least.'

Jesus took his dinner with all sorts of people;
people who were looked down on by others,
like Matthew in today's gospel.
And Matthew wasn't the first like that
whom he associated with.
Jesus seems to be at his best
when he's with people at their worst.

Like when you watch your child trying to walk and
        falling,
or a boy or girl in school really trying to learn something,
your heart goes out to them in their efforts,
and you really love them at that moment,
when they seem weakest, most vulnerable,
and they think they're inadequate.

When you're down, you feel God is down on you;
when you are giving out to yourself, you think God is
        doing the same;
when you feel empty inside, you think God is far away.

Like he's present in this small piece of bread at Mass,
he's present to you at the best and the worst of times.
Trust him;
be really present to him
as he's really present to you,
in Eucharist,
in love,
in every moment of every day.

ELEVENTH SUNDAY IN ORDINARY TIME

He had compassion on the crowd.

People were never just a crowd to Jesus.
He looked over the large crowd,
felt sorry for them,
and looked for help.

In any crowd that Jesus saw
were the sick and the lonely,
the mourners and the grieving,
the jobless and the poor;
and it is the same today,
we're all in that crowd.

He had compassion on the crowd.

Parents and children,
the old and the young.

But we're never a crowd to Jesus;
we're individuals,
each with our own personality,
our own gifts and talents,
our own sufferings and conflicts,
each with the hurts we bear in our hearts.

He fed the crowds then,
as he nourishes us now:
strengthening us and healing us
with the bread of the Son of God.
He taught them with the light of the Spirit,
and shared with all the compassion of the Father.

He had compassion on the crowd.

TWELFTH SUNDAY IN ORDINARY TIME

No love wasted

Love is like a bridge between heaven and earth.
When we try to love,
to care for another,
to look out for another in trouble,
to rear and raise a family in love,
then we are in the environment of God.

When God looks on a life,
He sees the field sown with love.
He sees that we dug and planted,
we watered and we fertilised our land,
we tended our field of love as best we could.

Hasn't many a parent spent years of effort in love,
and not been as successful as he wanted?
Hasn't many a teacher cared for generations of children,
and wonders what has been the fruit?

Husband, wives, parents, grandparents,
lives lived in the effort to love;
friendship, community, caring professions,
efforts to love, to care, to grow.

Not always successful.
Selfishness enters the field of love –
we need to be loved ourselves,
or we can't keep the effort going.

God sees the effort,
like he has counted the hairs of our heads,
like he sees his Son in bread and wine.

What's spent and offered in love
is never wasted
in the circle of love
which is God.

On the bridge between heaven and earth,
the bridge of love,
no effort is lost,
no kindness unnoticed,
no love wasted.

THIRTEENTH SUNDAY IN ORDINARY TIME

Anyone who prefers father, mother, son or daughter to me is not worthy of me.

> Maybe Jesus seems very self-important
> when he says that nothing must be preferred to him.
> You cannot prefer mother or father,
> son or daughter,
> or your own life,
> over Jesus.
>
> Surely he is not devaluing
> family relations,
> or life itself.
>
> Maybe it's something like this –
> that even the most valued things of life –
> family and life itself –
> are not as lasting as his friendship.
>
> Son or daughter can leave you, may die;
> so may father and mother,
> brother, sister, friend;
> but Jesus lasts,
> Word of God,
> Son of God,
> Bread of Life.

Anyone who prefers father, mother, son or daughter to me is not worthy of me.

FOURTEENTH SUNDAY IN ORDINARY TIME

In the ordinary

Come to a quiet place,
a place so quiet
that you can hear
the grass grow.
Run your fingers
through the softness
of its petals,
and listen:
listen to the earth,
the warm earth,
the life pulse
of us all.
Rest your body
against its warmth;
feel its greatness,
the pulse and throb,
the foundation
of the world.
Look up into the sky,
the all-embracing sky,
the canopy of heaven.
How small we really are:
specks in the greatness
but still a part of it all.
We grow from the earth
and find
our own place.

Anon

FIFTEENTH SUNDAY IN ORDINARY TIME

The seed fell on rich soil.

In the rich soil of care,
the word of God takes root.

In the fruitful soil of birth,
the word of God becomes flesh.

In the thorny soil of suffering,
the word of God consoles.

In the flowering soil of friendship,
the word of God makes sense.

In the deep soil of faith,
the word of God comes to life.

And in the times
we till our lives
with care, compassion,
with courage and endurance,
with joy and with love,
the word of God is sown by Jesus,
and bears its rich fruit,
and is given to us
in the Bread of Life.

The seed fell on rich soil.

SIXTEENTH SUNDAY IN ORDINARY TIME

Let them both grow till harvest time.

There's a bit of bad in the best of us,
and a lot of good in the worst of us.

How true.
Like the farmer in the gospel looking at weeds and wheat
      in a field,
we look at the goodness and the sinfulness in our lives.

People's strengths have their own weaknesses:
a generous person is often hot-tempered
and a placid person may seem cold or unfeeling.

Weeds and wheat, weeds and flowers, all grew in the
      farmer's field,
and God saw more of the colour and the growth than the
      weeds.
Same with you and me.

With God's grace and our co-operation
the good can overcome the bad.
And when God looks at a life,
he sees the life totally,
and the bad is lost and forgiven in the good.

And the word of God is patience.
Let them both grow till harvest time, he said,
otherwise, if you cut everything, you will do violence to
      the field.

Lord, help me to be patient with myself,
let me know that you see the heart
and you see that behind every fault and sin,
there is also the struggle to do good.

Let them both grow till harvest time.

SEVENTEENTH SUNDAY IN ORDINARY TIME

Like treasure hidden in a field

Where is the Kingdom of God?
How to recognise it?
Has it an anthem like a country,
a flag like a nation,
a language of its own?

In the middle of the heart of experience is found
the Kingdom of God.
Through the gaps of life,
shines the Kingdom of God.
Like treasure hidden in a field.

Glimpsed in the narrow gaps
between tight thoughts
and you're surprised by a new idea.
Glimpsed in the narrow gaps
between people who know each other
and you're surprised by the newness of one you love.
Glimpsed in the narrow gap
of acceptance of injustice and inequality,
and you're surprised by new initiatives.

There is no flag, no anthem, no language
separate from
the flag, anthem and language
of our experience of life:
the flag, anthem and language
of love, compassion, truth
of the works of justice,
of Eucharist.

Like treasure hidden in a field

EIGHTEENTH SUNDAY IN ORDINARY TIME

He saw a large crowd and had compassion on them.

A saint, Catherine of Siena, once said,
'Where we see faults, God sees struggles.'
You see people differently with the eye of compassion.

When Jesus saw the crowd without food
he asked only *how to feed them.*
No complaint as to
why they had come without food,
their lack of plans,
not even a suggestion of impatience.

In poverty Jesus never asks why you're poor,
his heart goes out to your poverty.
His heart goes out to the unemployed person,
not first asking why you have no job.
His heart goes out to the single parent
without question, without comment.
Or with sins, the first movement of the heart of Christ
is to forgive, to be compassionate, in relation with you.

He saw a large crowd and had compassion on them.

A marriage going badly,
a relationship being abused,
a conflict with parents,
Jesus sees the suffering of the heart,
and wants to help.

He gives that sense of wholeness,
never judging a person on one aspect of personality.
Faults are struggles,
and in knowing you're fully known and accepted,
you can accept the bread of strength
and move on stronger, whole, loved.
He saw a large crowd and had compassion on them.

NINETEENTH SUNDAY IN ORDINARY TIME

Courage, it is I! Do not be afraid.

When you fear for the future of your children, and
wonder will they make it safely through life,
Do not be afraid.

When you fear that love may not last and your
commitment will run dry,
Do not be afraid.

When you fear in teenage years that you'll not find
friends and you will be left alone,
Do not be afraid.

When death is close and you feel so confused and
anxious,
Do not be afraid.

When God seems distant and you can't find consolation,
Do not be afraid.

When faults and sin take over and you wonder can God
ever really love you,
Do not be afraid.

In all the moments of life
when it seems like walking on water,
in our fears and anxieties,
our despair and our hopelessness,
in mourning and sadness,
and also in joy and hope,
love and peace,
when the water is calm
and life seems to support us,
we hear the word of God:

Courage, it is I! Do not be afraid.

TWENTIETH SUNDAY IN ORDINARY TIME

A woman who was true to herself

Be true to yourself and your feelings,
Follow your heart and be guided by your mind;
Love sincerely and with respect;
express faithfully your love.
Listen and remember,
You're not alone.

Keep sight of your roots,
the love of your parents, your home, your friends.
these roots are only the beginnings.
You create the branches,
care for the fruit
and delight in the harvest.

Live really and honestly,
dream of peace and beauty,
Love gently and with care.
Have faith in God.

Be true to yourself.

John McHugh

TWENTY-FIRST SUNDAY IN ORDINARY TIME

You are Peter and on this rock I will build my Church.

'He must be joking', the others thought
when Jesus said,
'You are Peter and on this rock I will build my Church'.

They knew him well.
A rather mediocre fisherman,
a hot-tempered husband and father,
the centre of everything going on,
but could you rely on him?

They wouldn't be surprised later
that he would deny that he knew Jesus,
or that he would run away when the going was tough.

What they didn't think of
was that they would all run away as well!

Jesus saw into Peter's heart,
recognised his generosity,
his enthusiasm for a cause,
his love for family and friends,
and named him 'Rock'.

Maybe he recognised also that Peter
knew his faults and failings and weaknesses;
and isn't that a great security in life –
to know yourself well;
and that's what makes good leaders.

On the rock of Peter, Jesus built his Church,
and his Church is little different from Peter:
strong at times or weak,
enthusiastic and courageous,
sinful and unreliable,

for his Church is you and me,
our parish community,
the community of God's people,
confessing with joy
that Jesus is the Christ of God.

TWENTY-SECOND SUNDAY IN ORDINARY TIME

This must not happen to you:
For those who want to save their life will lose it,
and those who lose their life for my sake will find it.

> So often we think or say –
> it must not happen,
> it should not have happened.

> I must not fail an exam,
> I must get on better with my family,
> I must keep a strong faith,
> this love should not have failed,
> he should have lived longer,
> and you can add your own
> 'I must not'… or 'it should not…',
> when things are not going right.

> For Jesus knew he must go towards Calvary,
> towards giving himself to us in this death-way.
> For Peter it was unthinkable,
> this God-man, this Heaven-Friend,
> being led like a lamb to slaughter.

This must not happen to you:
For those who want to save their life will lose it,
and those who lose their life for my sake will find it.

> Are there not new ways of seeing life?
> Failure is not the end of life's journey,
> and may lead to some new strength in a person;
> love which dies may be renewed elsewhere later.
> All of life's happenings,
> chosen or not chosen –
> challenge us to trust in the goodness of God and life.

All are part of the 'saving ' and full development
of each person's unique, God-given personality.

This must not happen to you:
For those who want to save their life will lose it,
and those who lose their life for my sake will find it.

TWENTY-THIRD SUNDAY IN ORDINARY TIME

A prayer for every day

> Day after day, O Lord of my life,
> shall I stand before you face to face.
> With folded hands, O Lord of all worlds,
> shall I stand before you face to face.
>
> Under your great sky
> in solitude and silence,
> with humble heart,
> shall I stand before you face to face.
>
> In this laborious world of yours,
> busy with toil and trouble,
> among hurrying crowds,
> shall I stand before you face to face.
>
> And when my work shall be done in this world,
> O King of Kings,
> alone and speechless,
> shall I stand before you face to face.

Tagore

A prayer for every day

> This is my prayer to you, my Lord –
> strike, strike at the root of penury in my heart.
>
> Give me the strength lightly to bear my joys and sorrows.
> Give me the strength to make my love fruitful in service.
> Give me the strength never to disown the poor
> or bend my knees before greed and might.

Give me the strength to raise my mind high above daily
trifles.
And give me the strength to surrender my strength to
your will with love.

Tagore

TWENTY-FOURTH SUNDAY IN ORDINARY TIME

Forgiving others

The heart of God is a compassionate heart;
understanding weakness,
covering over faults and selfishness
and forgiving sins.

Compassion awaits compassion:
if God is compassionate to you,
surely you are to be compassionate to others.

Compassion opens the heart;
you see a person sleeping rough
and you wince and say
'it shouldn't be like that',
and you feel something deep inside for a person.
Compassion may often not be able to do anything
but offer presence, sympathy, support.

How often must I forgive others?

Or when someone doesn't hold your faults against you,
your heart is opened wider
and compassion enters
into the place forgiveness prepares.

Give thanks this day
for those who understand you;
give thanks this day
for those who forgive you;
give thanks this day
for those whom you understand and forgive.

And then the Eucharist
will more deeply touch your life,
for the Bread of God
is the bread baked with compassion.

How often must I forgive others?

TWENTY-FIFTH SUNDAY IN ORDINARY TIME

My ways are not your ways,
my thoughts are not your thoughts.

Don't we know this so well,
my ways are not your ways,
my thoughts are not your thoughts.

This is a big statement of faith.
We believe this because we know it
from failure, sickness, death, bereavement.

But to trust –
that is something more challenging.

Can I trust as a loved one is in a terminal illness
and I wonder why God does not call home?
Can I trust when a child is ill and we can't get at the
    cause?
Can I trust when love breaks up?

My ways are not your ways,
my thoughts are not your thoughts.

There are times when all we can say,
all we can remember,
all we can find hope in
is that on the cross of Calvary,
Jesus heard those same words,
and trusted in God his Father.

My ways are not your ways,
my thoughts are not your thoughts.

TWENTY-SIXTH SUNDAY IN ORDINARY TIME

The love of God for all

To accept that God first loved us,
through no merits of our own,
and that God is always there for us,
although we forget God,
is more difficult for us
than following God's commandments.

To accept that God loves us just as we are,
unconditionally, gratuitously, and forever,
is more difficult for us
than to sacrifice as we should for God and for others.

To accept that God forgives absolutely
and does not hold our past against us
is more difficult for us
than to repent of the evil we have done.

To accept this love of God
is the only path to freedom and interior peace.
And it is the underlying reason
why we should accept each other
and love each other just as we are.

Segundo Galilea, The Music of God

TWENTY-SEVENTH SUNDAY IN ORDINARY TIME

The stone the builders rejected has become the keystone

They rejected Jesus;
crucified his body and thought they killed his spirit;
and he still lives on,
in the hearts of millions,
in the Eucharist of each day.

Who are the strong ones of the kingdom of God?
What stone will keep together every other stone?

Doesn't a family often notice
that the weakest –
maybe the ill or the old or the handicapped –
keep the rest of us together?

Or maybe the ones who bring us closest to God
are the ones who need God most and know
the meaning and the joy of the mystery of needing God.

Would we know of Mother Teresa
if we didn't know of those who die alone
on our city streets?

The cross is a throne
and the man nailed to it
by the fear and pride of his creatures
is the biggest name and influence
the world has ever known.

Notice this week
whom you reject, belittle, or look down on;
they may be keystones
in the building of God's kingdom.

Notice this week
what in yourself
you reject,or belittle, or look down on:
they may be the keystones
of the kingdom of God in you.

TWENTY-EIGHTH SUNDAY IN ORDINARY TIME

On this mountain the Lord will prepare a banquet for all people.

We are here this day
at God's invitation.

There is no VIP section,
no conditions for being invited,
he has prepared his banquet
his Eucharist,
for all peoples.

The only condition is that we want to be here,
that we know our need for God,
our need to be nourished by the Bread of Life,
to be forgiven by the Word of God,
and then we are sent to be this Bread of Life.

This bread is baked, blessed,
broken, and shared
in the name of Jesus,
as the bread of life
was baked, blessed,
broken and shared by his disciples.

Nourish us, Lord Jesus,
with the bread that satisfies
our hunger for meaning and direction in our lives,
our thirst for a companionship that is always faithful,
our hope for the fullness of forgiveness,
our deep need to know we are totally loved.

No conditions for joining in this banquet;
come to God as you are,
and you will return
blessed, refreshed, strengthened
and sent forth in his name.

TWENTY-NINTH SUNDAY IN ORDINARY TIME

Being thankful

Let's be thankful
for the simple things of life;
for what is ordinary and everyday,
for what we take for granted.

Qualities of the body like health and energy,
personal qualities like courage in any problems;
for food and for shelter,
for friendships and love in life.

Can we be grateful also
for what tries us in life,
like failure and let-down,
loss and downheartedness?
For it may deepen our love
and our appreciation of life.

Let's be grateful for faith and for prayer,
for the closeness of God in sacrament and love;
for the meaning in life
which comes from faith, family and love.
It's good to be thankful,
it keeps us humble and we know our place:
that so much we have is from others.

For what we cannot now be grateful,
for the conflicts and what seems impossible in our lives,
we offer in prayer and hope to God,
knowing that he lives our life to the full.

Thanks is the big word of our Mass,
for Eucharist means thanks.
Let's offer the care we give to others
as a way of saying thanks to God.

THIRTIETH SUNDAY IN ORDINARY TIME

There are only two commandments:
love God and love your neighbour.

> Hasn't Jesus made it a bit too simple?
> Loving God – what a question!
> Loving who or what?
> Loving what I cannot see,
> the cause of all that moves,
> the source of all life.

> That would be remote,
> frightening, distant.

> Isn't it simpler to say:
> what you love in another, you love in God.
> When you love another, you love God.

> **There are only two commandments:**
> **love God and love your neighbour.**

> Loving your child is loving God;
> loving your husband or wife is loving God;
> loving a pupil, a friend,
> loving one you cannot stand,
> this is loving God.

> And in the evening of our lives,
> we'll remember back
> to whom we loved and tried to love,
> we will dance with joy for those we loved,
> and ask forgiveness of someone,
> of God, of others, of life,
> for those we hurt.

We know deep down in our good hearts,
that in fact Jesus was right.
He was not simple
but challenging us to the most difficult thing in life:

There are only two commandments:
love God and love your neighbour.

THIRTY-FIRST SUNDAY IN ORDINARY TIME

You have only one teacher: Jesus Christ.

> Sometimes a teacher may bend down to speak to a small
> child,
> or share an experience of loneliness or love with a young
> person;
> teaching from within the group,
> knowing what we are like,
> and guiding us a few steps further on the way.
> Jesus teaches like this,
> for he is like us in all things but sin.

You have only one teacher: Jesus Christ.

> All of life is learning:
> the simplest of activities like eating and drinking,
> the most complicated like learning a language,
> mastering the computer.

> And there are other lessons:
> we learn to trust from our family,
> and from God through people
> we learn to love, forgive, be compassionate,
> we learn to care for others,
> stay faithful to partners and to community,
> and we learn how to suffer, bear pain,
> and eventually we learn to die.

> In the bread of the Eucharist
> is the life of the One
> who is the teacher, the Truth.

> From the word of God,
> spoken through the experiences of many people,
> we learn what is best in life:
> meaning, direction, fullness.

From this word we learn also
how to live, in the fullest way possible,
the way of Jesus Christ.

You have only one teacher: Jesus Christ.

THIRTY-SECOND SUNDAY IN ORDINARY TIME

They brought oil as well as their lamps

> We are each the light of God;
> a light given with the candle given to our parents in
>   baptism,
> the light of faith
> to guide our steps in the way of Jesus,
> to enlighten our minds in the truth of Jesus,
> to nourish our love with the life of Jesus.

> You are light,
> you are the lamp of God,
> and this light is the warmth of God.

> And the power of the lamp is the love of God.

> In the Eucharist our light is brightened,
> and the lamp is renewed,
> as a waterfall generates electricity,
> as love generates new life.

They brought oil as well as their lamps.

> Take time to refresh your spirit,
> take time for prayer,
> take time for Eucharist,
> take time for wonder,
> be surprised by God
> in the November sunrise,
> in the Christmas anticipation,
> in the evening's winter peace,
> and your light glows new again.

They brought oil as well as their lamps.

THIRTY-THIRD SUNDAY IN ORDINARY TIME

You entrusted me with two talents;
here are two more I have made.

> We are familiar with the story
> of the boy who wanted to bring a gift
> to Jesus at his birth.
> He saw others bringing expensive gifts
> of gold, frankincense and myrrh;
> he wondered what he had to offer,
> and thought of his drum,
> and how he could play a song
> for Jesus, Mary and Joseph.

> A simple story,
> and isn't it true about our gifts and talents?

> Each of us has different qualities, gifts:
> all are given by God
> and are valued in God's love:
> gifts of music, sport and art,
> of conversation and humour,
> of compassion and leadership;
> gifts of friendship, prayer and
> caring for others,
> of listening and encouraging;
> whatever your gift, your talent;
> your gift of being a caring parent,
> of being able to help a younger generation in any way;
> be grateful,
> each of us has a 'bit of God' within us;
> and each of us can offer to God
> in our love and care for others
> what he has given to us.

He looks on us, and loves each of us;
sees us as we are and loves us,
sees us as we can be
and calls each of us,
in our own personality and talents,
to grow in love,
to offer our talents in his service,
and to become more like him.

LAST SUNDAY IN ORDINARY TIME
CHRIST THE KING

Whatever you do for the least of my people, you do for me.

He is a king for the poor.
They say about him he was like a shepherd
who kept all his sheep in view,
like a teacher keeping an eye on every student in the class,
like a parent giving time to all the children,
a grandparent remembering each grandchild.
All are important,
especially the lost, the strays, the wounded and the weak.

And when he meets us all in the final kingdom
he'll wonder how we treated the weak, the lost and the
     poor.
Strange type of king;
not a collector of taxes,
not the richest one in the land,
not the one defended by his people,

but the generous one,
the one who was poor
and the one who defended his own to death.

And how do we honour him?
His own words say it all:
Whatever you do for the least of my people,
you do for me.

THE IMMACULATE CONCEPTION

Mary, you are blessed

Blessed are you, Mary,
happy in your searching for and finding
the truth and word of God within you.

And you are blessed
because you knew you were helpless
and only God could give you
the life your soul looked for.

And blessed are you,
for your life was poor in spirit, gentle;
blessed are you for you could mourn and laugh,
and make peace among people.

And you are blessed in your pain
of giving your son back to God.

Blessed are you when you heard the grief of Jesus'
    disciples;
and blessed are you when you heard their joys.
blessed are you when you taught them to pray;
Blessed are you in meeting your risen Son, face to face,
and within the community of the disciples
he left in your care.

Blessed are you,
and we praise you,
Mary, mother of God,
pray for us, sinners,
now and at the hour of our death.
Amen.

THE EPIPHANY OF THE LORD

And they returned to their country by a different way.

They had journeyed
for weeks, maybe months,
through desert, towns,
all sorts of weather.

Expecting to find a king,
and as we know,
they found a child.
Expecting to find a palace,
and as we know,
they found a stable.
Expecting to find royalty,
and as we know,
they found Mary and Joseph.

Surprised by God,
surprised by life,
isn't that how it is for us all?

Surprised by Christmas?
An idea in a homily or a radio talk,
the moments of prayer when God seemed close,
the child's surprise gift or smile,
the lift in the heart of a spouse's love?

Or the opposite?
The phone call that never came,
the loneliness of being on your own,
the memories of other Christmasses, that bring pain,
the doubt that God is near at all.

Like for the Magi,
the journey was the best of times, the worst of times.
But the star always guided them,
never within grasp,
always within sight.

Maybe we travel into the same places
but by a different way
because of the birth of Christ.

The child of Bethlehem reminds each of us
that we are loved children of God
and that each of us has our star,
never within grasp,
always within the sight of faith,
guiding us into the light of God.

SAINT PATRICK

Christ be with me

Christ be with me, Christ within me,
Christ behind me, Christ before me,
Christ beside me, Christ to win me,
Christ to comfort and restore me.
Christ beneath me, Christ above me,
Christ in quiet, Christ in danger,
Christ in hearts of all that love me,
Christ in mouth of friend and stranger.

Christ in every home and friendship,
Christ in every school and workplace.
Christ in all our people elsewhere,
Christ in all who left our land.
Christ in all our hopes for peace,
Christ in all our work for peace.
Christ in all our hopes for justice.
Christ in all our work for justice.

Christ with all our young and old,
Christ with all our sick and dying.
Christ with all who mourn and sorrow,
Christ with the lonely and forgotten.
Christ with all who taught us faith,
Christ with all who shared their hope,
Christ with all who gave us love,
Christ with all in heaven's joy.

THE ASCENSION OF THE LORD

Why are you standing here, looking into the sky?

It's a strange sort of parting,
the feast of the Ascension.
It looks as if Jesus is gone forever.
As if the word made flesh is now
the human flesh become a divine spirit.

And his friends looked into the sky,
lost, bereft, confused,
because he said he would be with them,
all days even to the end of time.

It's a strange sort of parting,
because it's a new sort of presence.

Listen to what he had said:

where two or three are gathered in my name
there I am among you,

those who eat my flesh and drink my blood
live in me and I in them,

I make my home in you,
make your home in me.

And these are statements of presence,
the real presence of Jesus
in love,
in sacrament,
in friendship.

Why are you standing here, looking into the sky?
For the Lord we seek is among us.

THE BODY AND BLOOD OF CHRIST

The bread that I shall give is my flesh, for the life of the world

Isn't the greatest gift
one can give to another,
the gift of oneself?

Gifts can be sent in the post,
credited and impersonally given;
a gift can be chosen quickly or with care.
the gift expressing the giver's personality
or the relationship between two people
is most welcomed.

That's the gift of the Eucharist;
**The bread that I shall give is my flesh,
for the life of the world.**

This means, it is myself.

When I give my time and listen,
when I share my experience,
or speak from the heart,
or risk opening myself
that another person may grow,
then I am giving myself,

and this is what Jesus does.

He allows us into the hidden heart of his life:
his relationship with his Father,
his real beliefs about love and justice,
peace and religion, life and death;

his hopes for the poor,
his conviction to suffer and die
for God and for us.

He breaks the joys and sorrows of his life,
he invites his disciples and friends –
you and me –
to share our love
for the life and growth,
the encouragement and development
of those with whom we share our lives.

**The bread that I shall give,
is my flesh for the life of the world.**

THE ASSUMPTION OF MARY

Emmanuel: God is with you!

The promise made to Mary in her youth:
the Son born of you will be named Emmanuel,
which means 'God is with us'.

She could look back in her old age
at the mystery of God being with her,
throughout all her life.

In pregnancy, as she awaited the birth of Jesus,
she was graced with the support of Joseph and Elizabeth;
in birth, when her Son was born in poverty,
she saw that some rejected, some received him,
even at that early age.

And she experienced the death of her husband
and God was with her then,
as Jesus and friends consoled her.

And she let Jesus go,
the Son whom she loved,
to his work for God
which involved her
only in a hidden way.

She watched him die,
and he gave her then
to his disciples and to the Church;
'Be their mother', he said;
'This is your Son', as he gave her to John,
and she gave him back to God.

And in old age,
like all of us,
she looked back, and recognised

that God was always faithful,
God was always with her.

She brought God to us
in the Word made flesh;
and now God welcomes her home,
fully alive in his presence.

As she now is,
we one day shall be.
Thanks be to God!

ALL SAINTS

The feast of the 'ordinary' Christian

In many cities of the world
you may visit the tomb of the Unknown Soldier.
This commemorates the millions
who were the ordinary soldiers
who died, heroically and tragically, in war.

An altar to the unknown saint
would be a fitting commemoration
in our churches
for the millions of ordinary Christians
and who lived lives of quiet,
often strong and heroic sanctity.

We think this day
of our unknown saints,
known only to those
whose lives they touched.
We have been made who we are
by their love and their faith.

For our grandparents, for our parents,
first teachers of faith,
first givers of love, we give thanks this day;
For our family,
brothers and sisters, and extended family,
with whom we shared much of life,
we give thanks this day;
For teachers, priests,
sisters, brothers,
all who guided our schooling,
often with little personal reward,
we give thanks this day;
And for others whose Christian life
has influenced our own faith in God,
we give thanks this day.